LARRY
on Larry

Terence Parkes
with Mark Bryant

A Mark Bryant Book
GRUB STREET · LONDON

Published by Grub Street, The Basement,
10 Chivalry Road, London SW11 1HT

Text copyright © 1994 Terence Parkes & Mark Bryant
Cartoons copyright © 1994 Terence Parkes

The moral right of the authors has been asserted

A catalogue record of this book is available from the
British Library

ISBN: 0 948817 86 0

Printed and bound in Great Britain by
Biddles Ltd, Guildford and King's Lynn

ACKNOWLEDGEMENTS

Some of the cartoons in this book originally appeared in *Punch,
Private Eye, Opera Now* and the *Oldie* and are reproduced with the
kind permission of those publications. Photographs on page 7 and 18
are reproduced by kind permission of Verulamium Museum, St
Albans, and Times Newspapers, respectively, and many thanks to
Elfa Kramers and the late Michael ffolkes for permission to use the
cartoon on page 128.

This book is dedicated to the British Post Office workers who have been
moving my cartoons around for years. They get no praise – but here's
some from me. It's been my experience that they never fail to get
work delivered to its destination. And such times as cartoons have got
lost it's been the customer who's lost them. In particular, praise for my
local sub-postmaster – he even licks and sticks my stamps on for me.

INTRODUCTION

I WAS BORN in Birmingham, near Villa Park football stadium, on Saturday 19 November 1927. I don't remember who Aston Villa were playing at home that day but there must have been a good crowd as a huge cheer was heard at the adjoining maternity hospital at four o'clock, coinciding with my arrival in this world (my mother swore blind it had nothing to do with Villa scoring).

The speed of life being what it is, before I knew what had hit me I reached the age of five and was bundled off to the local Brum infants' school – St Peter's in Harbourne. Unbeknown to me, a mere ink-pellet's flick away stood the house of the celebrated watercolour painter, David Cox. But who knows? Maybe the presence of this great man's shade only a few yards' distant began to shuffle my latent artistic genes into some sort of order. I certainly remember drawing a rather attractive tattoo – two hearts spliced by a dagger – on my left arm in Stephens permanent blue-black ink with a dip pen. My satisfaction was short-lived, however – Grannie Wilson the headmistress obviously felt that every true artist must also suffer for his work and caned me on my drawing hand.

My earliest preserved drawing is one I did at the age of six when I produced a portrait of myself with a model aeroplane – the kind you shot into the air with a catapult (it came free with *Chips* comic, I seem to recall). 'Here is me flying my heroplane' it was entitled. Not bad

spelling for a lad of six – the trouble is it hasn't improved much since, which may be another reason why I don't use many captions in my cartoons these days.

Partly, perhaps, because of Grannie Wilson's dedication to her particular régime of physical treatment to develop my artistic abilities but mostly because of a diet of Tizer, crisps and Mars bars, I grew into a chunky sort of lad, as can be seen in a snapshot of me taken at about this time. This was in the autumn of 1939, three days before war started. The other fellow in the picture is my schoolmate Vernon Frost (now a retired civil servant), and we were then in our second year at Dennis Howell's old school, Handsworth Grammar, which had been evacuated to Stroud in Gloucestershire. We had been billeted on an elderly childless couple but Vernon and I didn't get on at first and Mr and Mrs Bray got fed up with us always scrapping and slung us out after a few months. So we were shunted off to a big house for the throw-outs and general 'bad lots' (mostly 15- to 16-year-olds) called

Me and Vernon Frost (with the cap) aged 12.

'Northfields' where we learnt how to smoke, play cards and avoid washing. Later we were bundled off again, this time to Mr and Mrs Wilson, a childless couple who were rich and lived in a lovely Georgian house. But with the fall of France all the parents panicked, had us brought back to Birmingham and reopened the school. And then came the air-raids. One bomb made a huge crater in the school pitch and in November 1941 an aerial mine blew out all the windows, which meant a month's holiday. Three cheers for Hitler!

I began well enough at school but never managed better than thirteenth in class. However, I was good at Art but in those days if you were in the 'A' stream you had to do Latin instead. So I dropped down a stream (I found this fairly easy to do). Then, at the age of 15, after taking my School Certificate to get out of having to act in the school play, I got two days' leave to sit the entrance exam for Birmingham School of Art. To my amazement I passed and spent a very happy three years discovering the pleasures of Life Studies –

especially drawing the female nude, of course. We also drew from the Antique – plaster casts of the Venus de Milo, the Belvedere Torso and the Boy with a Dolphin. The boy with the fish came to a sad end when I had a scrap with a lad named Snowdon. In the tussle we piled into the cast and totally wrecked it. Somehow we got off with a prolonged earful from the Principal – no more. We should have been expelled, but that was what was so nice about Art School.

This period in my education was interrupted by two years' National Service (1946-8). I was in the Royal Artillery in camps in Wales and Barnard Castle, Durham, and then got transferred to Portsmouth where there was nothing to do except drink and be merry. From what I remember we spent most of the time lumbering about in giant umpteen-tonner trucks, picking up fish-and-chips and beer from the town and ferrying them back to the camp. I also remember keeping my hand in by helping Gunner John Mason do a mural on the wall of the Officers'

An early *Punch* cartoon, 1953.

4

'You know I still don't believe you're one of these 'ere Glorious Gloucesters!'

Mess in 1947, and then it was back to art college. This time we had the advantage of a Government grant for interrupted schooling of £3 a week – a tidy sum in those days and almost twice our service pay. Ever the realist, I decided to opt for book illustration as my special study rather than 'fine' art proper. Our great influences at the time were Eric Bawden and Edward Ardizzone – I was in the Diz team. I was also starting to doodle out a few cartoons – for the very practical reason that when it came to getting some of your work published it looked like the most achievable goal. I touted my wares to the *Birmingham Gazette* and to my delight managed to sell a few, signed in those days with my real name.

Then it was back to reality. The course I was on was designed to produce art teachers for the newly formed Secondary Modern Schools and I found myself in the last kind of job that I would ever have imagined myself ending up in: teaching the kids of Perkins Diesel factory-workers in Peterborough. This was in 1950. Mind you, the pay wasn't bad – £750 a year with an increment of £250 as a specialist teacher was a fair amount in those days – about the same as a GP was getting. And to be fair it was quite a good school. However, the Head didn't appreciate my teaching methods, which instead of using neat exercise books involved the kids splashing paint everywhere. I tried to justify the mess by claiming that the classroom looked like a proper artists' studio. But the Head was not convinced: 'Tell that to the cleaners,' he said.

After about three years I chucked it in and went back to Birmingham to work in the Lucas Turbines factory as a progress-chaser. It was a very large factory and the great advantage

My first cartoon for *Lilliput*, 1954

of my job was that I was able to swan about all over the place 'chasing progress' and nobody would give a tinker's cuss where you were. As a result I spent hours at a time thinking up ideas for cartoons and scribbling them down on company notepaper in the loo or behind packing cases, and drawing them up at night.

Meanwhile, I'd married an old college flame, Pauline, in 1952. Herself a smashing artist, it's a wonder my work practices at this time didn't lead to instant divorce. Apart from constantly pestering her about her opinion of my latest cartoons as they came off the production line – often at midnight – I also had the irritating habit of dropping drawings onto the floor to dry. Naturally houseproud, this drove her potty and when she brought in a cup of tea she would frequently pretend not to see the pile of finished artwork and 'accidentally'

tramp over it. Since then I've never let her near one of my drawings (and anyway, she's more of a fan of Mac of the *Daily Mail*).

So, back to the plot. Still working at Lucas I kept banging away at various newspapers and magazines and eventually got my first cartoon published in *Punch* in 1954. Then by a miracle, just before the birth of my son in 1956, I managed to land a staff job as a cartoonist on the *Daily Express* – a proper job at last! But it would be short-lived. Sharing a cubicle squeezed between political cartoonist Michael Cummings and sports cartoonist Roy Ullyett I never did get my own desk. And it was a tough place to find yourself – all simmering hatred between rival features journalists, nearly coming to blows as they argued about their positions on the page. It all amazed me, but not for long – I was given the Order of the Boot after only three months and so it was back to factories.

My one and only *Punch* cover, 1 August 1979

Trying to look like a Roman Emperor at Verulamium Museum, St Albans, 1990.

as they really are and send everyone off to sleep. My wife, Pauline, and Gerda, my gentle Rottweiler, have checked the proofs for anything they don't like the look of and all the jolly people at Grub Street Publishing have worked very hard to make sure it looks a damn sight tidier than the suitcase full of doodles, blots and scribblings that I presented them with when they expressed an interest in doing the thing.

I was going to call it all 'Why do I bother' or some such title, but then I thought, bugger it, why bother even that much – let them choose a title. So anyway here it is – a sort of version of my life in cartoons over the last 40 years or so. All things considered, it's not been a bad time, but don't ask me what it all means. As far as I'm concerned, I've had a few laughs, swilled a few pints and met some smashing people. And after all's said and done it certainly beats working for a living.

Larry

However, within a year I found that the cartoons I was able to think up in the works lav were appearing regularly enough in the *Daily Sketch*, *Express* and *Punch* to make me think I could go it alone as a cartoonist. So in 1957 I took the plunge and set up shop on my own. I've never been employed since. And the rest, as they say, is history.

The remaining pages of this little book, then, fill in a bit more about the kinds of things I've been up to in my life as a cartoonist. With the help of Mark Bryant, who was daft enough to get me rambling on in the first place, I've mucked about with the order of the pictures and words a bit so that they don't all look as boring

LARRY AT HOME

Around 1960 the idea of husbands washing up and doing housework was pretty novel (some might say it still is!). Mostly it was the younger generation of middle-class males and the joke behind it all, I suppose, was when the older blokes started trying to be 'new men' as well. Russell Brockbank, then Art Editor of *Punch*, suggested I take on the subject and the upshot was a series of caption-less cartoons called 'Man in Apron'.

To my surprise it really caught on and collections of the drawings were even published in the USA, earning praise from such comic 'greats' as Charles 'Snoopy' Schultz and Harpo Marx.

I followed it up with a number of other

series all using this same character – Man in Garden, Man at Work, Man in Office and the like – and I suppose it is for these kind of gags (as well as the Art ones) that I'm best known.

This bloke I draw must somehow strike a familiar chord with readers. He's your average sort of middle-aged, middle-class husband. If he was

in a war he wouldn't be a great soldier – I can't see him charging. He's more like Bruce Bairnsfather's Old Bill – a survivor. He tends to get embarrassed about love and doesn't really know what it's all about, but he's reliable. He's not practical, of course, but he's ingenious, and he gets there in the end.

I've also drawn him in the bath quite a lot. I don't know why – it's not as if I think up my jokes in the bath or anything like that. And I've never personally come across any grown-up who makes a regular thing about playing with plastic ducks or toy aircraft-carriers in the tub. I suppose it must be about the child in the man, revealing something about him in the same way as stamps, model railways, radio-controlled model aeroplanes and matchstick buildings do. They're all in the same category, childish pursuits carried on by apparently normal people not obviously certifiable. But then again, I do remember on one occasion taking a bath after my young grandsons and enjoying playing with the plastic ships they left behind – bombing them with bars of soap and firing broadsides with Crazy Foam...

It's always said that cartoonists tend to draw their own self-portrait in cartoons, but my 'little man' character, if anybody, was based on my father. Indefatigable he was – though, like me, he always had a good head of hair. The reason I drew him bald was to distinguish him from the women – my cartoon faces always look the same, male or female.

Today, of course, there's nothing unusual in the husband doing the household chores or even tending the kids at home with the wife out at work – no laughs here any more. I remember watching the rot set in when we lived in Solihull in the late 1950s. Our bedroom window overlooked the kitchens of a row of modern houses. In every one you could see the husband cooking, washing up and even ironing – and half of them were hulking great blokes who played rugby for the local team. It's the same in my own family now. My son and son-in-law both wear pinafores and help around the home – though the new technology has spared them the joys of washing nappies...

As for myself, I think I must be one of the last of the 'old man' school before they broke the mould. Barely trusted with the washing up and with an innate resistance to hoovering. I tried cooking once. Working from a recipe book I somehow managed to warm up some steaks to a passable temperature but the dessert was a disaster – I forget what it was supposed to be but it ended up as a dark sticky mass of solid caramel which no known household gadget could scrape out of the fruit dishes for weeks!

9

Russell Brockbank

If I ever had a mentor I suppose it was Russell Brockbank. He was Art Editor of Punch *at the time I first began to sell cartoons and such was his influence on the magazine that I always felt he was actually level-pegging with the Editor, Bernard Hollowood. A rather irascible Canadian, he was famous for his brilliantly detailed motoring cartoons and was himself a crack driver. Such was his repute amongst the motoring fraternity that he would often be lent new models to try out and on one occasion drove the latest Jag from London to Penzance and back, non-stop, before starting work on a Monday.*

A kindly man, he would always add some useful comments to his rejection letters – in my case usually discouraging me from overdrawing, as he liked my quick scribbles just as they were. At my first meeting with him he asked me who my favourite cartoonist was and, thinking to please him, I replied 'Thelwell' who was Punch's *top artist at the time, along with Alex Graham and David Langdon. His expression suggested I'd made a mistake – 'Don't you like John Taylor?' Naturally I said I did and he continued praising the 'brevity' of the artist by contrast with Thelwell's detailed drawings. So it was Brockbank who really kept me on with my sketchy style, publishing drawings I originally sent in just as roughs and later commissioning the 'Man in Apron' series which gave me my first real success as a cartoonist.*

*I*t's a joke in itself my having done so many cartoons about gardening – these days all we've got is a small backyard, living as we do in the middle of Stratford. But it wasn't always so. Our previous house had a quarter of an acre to dig, weed and tend. I used to love all that dibbling and deadheading, muckspreading and mulching, not to mention lobbing snails over the fence and ambushing offending cats with the water hose. Happy days in an Indian summer as the bees buzzed, the finches trilled and the blackfly destroyed the last of my kidney beans.

But the part of gardening I really liked most was pruning: we used to have yards and yards of laurel hedgerow. And after the snipping and gathering there was the satisfaction of a huge bonfire at the end of the day. It made me a bit unpopular with the neighbours, though. I remember one occasion when the old boy a couple of doors away got furious after flakes of wood-ash blew a couple of hundred yards and pebbledashed his freshly painted rough-cast wall!

In my opinion the funniest side to gardening was and still is the visit to the garden centre to buy container-grown bits of plant and shrub. If you stroll round Solihull, West Midlands – not the most exciting tour to make, I grant you – you will see row upon row of neat front gardens all decked out with identical shrubs supplied by the same garden centre. In fact it some-times comes as a relief to spot the occasional concrete gnome or fake wishing-well. But it must be said, the good folk of Solihull keep themselves

smart, albeit with
precision-engineered uniformity.

Nowadays, restricted for space as we
are in Stratford, we've gone in for
water gardening. Old mixing bowls, a
cattle trough and various old tin tubs
lie scattered about the yard and it's
bliss – no weeding or feeding's needed
and the only garden tool required is a
hosepipe. Mind you, the mosquitoes
can be a bit of a problem, but the
frogs tend to keep them down and
the cat looks after the frogs...

Talking of small spaces, I did once
have a friend who was always going
through phases and for a
while was mad keen on

Bonsai gardening. Whenever we
met all he ever talked about was
miniature fruit trees and the wonders
of the Orient. It all came to an end
rather suddenly, though, when he
signed up for a residential weekend
course of lectures on the subject.
Something the Japanese horticultural
experts said must have driven him
to distraction for no sooner had he
arrived home than he slung the lot in
the dustbin and took up scuba-diving
instead!

We did have an allotment once – or
rather we shared one with a doctor
pal. But I never could understand
why his half always did better than
mine. His spuds always came up
bigger, his runner beans raced up the
poles and his marrows were like
Zeppelins. And then I caught him one
balmy June evening as the sun was
setting, pottering up and down a row
of beetroots and injecting them with
some evil-looking liquid in a hypoder-
mic syringe. It was then that I decided
to give up gardening and bought a
dog. So now we don't have much of
a garden – not even a lawn to mow.
I can't say I really miss it. But on an
autumn day the smell of a neighbour's bonfire can still
move me to tears (my
wife says it's just the
smoke getting in
my eyes).

Mr Punch's Last Gasp

It was a sad day for cartoonists when Punch *finally closed in 1992. It had been having apoplectic fits in an effort to keep up with the newly launched comic* Viz *and at the same time managed to estrange all the trad middle-of-the-road readership of solicitors, architects and doctors who were its mainstay (mind you, I never knew a dentist who took it) and had been for a century and a half. It had its final fling, ironically, at its 150th-anniversary celebrations the previous autumn. Hundreds of well-manicured bodies were packed Filofax to Vodaphone in the V&A Museum in a desperate effort to relaunch it by burning up all that remained of its scanty resources. But trying to find another cartoonist amongst the gaggle of freeloaders, advertising executives and men in grey suits was like trying to find a needle in a haystack. You could see the spirit of the magazine had already flown.*

One fun thing did come out of the 150th celebrations, though. A bunch of us were asked to produce a hand-decorated poster announcing the anniversary on a site near Vauxhall Bridge. Symptomatic, perhaps, of what has happening elsewhere in the magazine, it turned out that the hoarding they'd booked faced in the wrong direction – it was a one-way system and the only time anyone would see our handiwork would be in their rearview mirrors! After we'd finished mucking up this nice big sheet of paper I spotted a Lloyds Bank advert on the other side of the road. It featured a couple of rabbits in an enormous empty white space. We thought they looked a bit lonely and so Tony Husband, Paul Thomas and I crossed the street and filled a few more to keep them company. Now I come to think of it, this was probably the last job I did for Punch.

SCHOOL
RECORD

*A*h, schooldays! Grand times, great laughs. I remember the coconut mat we shoved in the piano just before morning assembly, the tunes we played on our bicycle pumps as the Head tried to deliver his boring speech on prize-giving day - those were magical moments.

But you get a very different perspective on school life if you end up teaching after having been an unruly pupil yourself as a lad. You can see the other chap's side of the conflict, as it were, once you've had to sit up there behind the big desk, chalk dust in your hair, willing your pupils to be creative and yet to stay quiet while they're about it.

When I started teaching in Peterborough in 1950, most of the staff were ex-servicemen who'd taken two-year crash courses after the war but had no degrees of other qualifications. It was a well-run school with an old-style late-Victorian disciplinarian head who soon got the former airmen and petty officers into shape, and on the whole the calibre of the staff (all male as it was a boys' school) was pretty high.

The one exception, of course, was yours truly. Previous to my appointment art had been delegated to non-specialist teachers who thought it was all about sitting the kids in straight rows and drawing tidy little pictures – high marks for those with the fewest smudges and a good report guaranteed to the boy who managed to make his HB pencil last the whole term. But I threw all that out the window. The first thing I did was to arrange the desks in two semi-circles, order huge tins of powder-paint in strident colours to replace the dainty little paintboxes and encourage my little Van Goghs to let rip.

It didn't really work out, though. The classes only lasted 40 minutes each which hardly gave enough time to sharpen pencils and unearth incomplete daubs from the previous session before the arduous process of removing paint from the walls and floor had to begin again. If I'd taken it at all seriously I would have gone mad. I chucked it in after three years. Schooldays the best years of your life? Bah! But it had its high moments. I remember painting this huge mural of rugby players on the wall of the canteen in one of the schools I taught at during my teaching practice. It went down well with the staff but the kids were totally non-plussed. What was this funny-shaped ball? No one had bothered to tell me it was a soccer-playing school!

Strip Cartoons

I didn't pursue the idea of producing a strip for very long. Years ago I did the early drawings for '4D Jones' – a combined effort with my old Birmingham school mate, Peter Maddocks – but I soon dropped out and he went on to make it a great success (it ran in the Express *for ten years). Then I worked with Frank Dickens on a take-off of the James Bond films called '008', featuring a charlady spy based at the British Embassy in Moscow. Confident that the secret-agent mania was just a passing phase the* Express *in their wisdom decided that it would date and dropped it – I've been gnashing my teeth ever since. But for all the crisp oncers (or even tenners) that I might have earnt from them, I never really felt a great urge to produce strips. Making room in the drawing for caption balloons always irked me. That said, though, I did once have a solo strip, 'The Slumps', about a working-class family batting around in the Middle Ages. It appeared in some long-defunct midweek paper –* Top Spot *I think it was called – at the end of 1959 and took up a whole page. Come to think of it, looking back at my cuttings, it probably contributed to the paper kicking the bucket.*

What sort of a landing does the family make ! We'll keep them suspended for you until next week!

September 12, 1959

Larry IN THE OFFICE

I've not had a lot of experience of working in an office. The only time I had a regular desk job was for a brief spell when I was on the staff of the *Daily Express*, and then I never actually had my own desk. I remember recognizing another cartoonist, Osbert Lancaster (he'd yet to be knighted), who had a patch on a communal desk in the Features Department which he shared with the leading women feature-writers. I didn't have the nerve to introduce myself but just sat quietly working on my window-sill, hardly breathing in his august company.

Lancaster was quite a dandy. Coming into the office immaculately tailored, he would take off his bowler hat, hand it with his umbrella to a copy boy and then sit at his drawing-board, flick a cuff to free his drawing hand and commence his daily pocket cartoon. Once, surveying the office at this juncture, he looked at me and said: 'With what shall we tickle the nation's ribs this morning?'

I did once, briefly, get a desk – or rather a part of a desk – when the tennis-writer was away for a week and I squeezed into his cubicle along with Michael Cummings and Roy Ullyett (there was never any sign of Giles in the building – he was allowed to work at home). It was a serious business working in that office – no talking or fraternization. But Roy Ullyett did once tell me 'You're doing well,

1955. It was during the Editor's absence from the office for an operation for piles or something. When he came out of hospital he decided to sack everyone he hadn't hired – which included me. As the Features chief said at the time: 'He wouldn't have done it if it hadn't been so near to Christmas.'

So that was the end of my office work and I've been self-employed ever since. I can't say I've missed it. The grubby office parties, furtive liaisons behind the filing cabinets, arguments over the photocopier or whose turn it is to make the coffee. No more cringing when the boss comes by, secret private phone calls on company time, interminable meetings and the inhuman crush on the Tube. But then again, I suppose there are the joys of paid holidays, sick leave, luncheon vouchers, nine-to-five work hours and . . . people to talk to. Maybe office life does have its compensations.

lad' – and made favourable comparisons with Gerard Hoffnung who had had my slot the previous year but couldn't stick it and left. Praise indeed, I thought. This was all at the end of

A Cultural Exchange

One rather oddball event, which was only vaguely connected with cartooning, took me behind the Iron Curtain to the Ukraine. For reasons best known to themselves, Central TV and Gostel TV in Kiev decided it would be interesting to film a cultural exchange between the good citizens of East and West and planned a programme featuring a straight swap between a policeman, a factory-worker etc, and, by some lunatic afterthought, a cartoonist.

While my opposite number, Yuri, evaded the organizers in England by disappearing down local hostelries (we're an international breed, cartoonists), I spent a happy week trying to keep my end of the bargain in Kiev, accompanied by a smart young interpreter, Alex Sheppel. While the factory-worker rubbed shoulders with his brothers in Soviet manufacturing and the bobby tramped the beat with Dmitri of Dock Greensk, I had a rare old time meeting Alex's mates, seeing the sights and testing the strengths of various amnesia-inducing brews that kept miraculously appearing every time my glass seemed empty.

One day I spent some time with the Kiev police. I asked them how much car crime they had and the chief told me they had a hatchback stolen a couple of Sundays ago – not much future in it for the average hoodlum as the scarcity of vehicles means they'd soon get caught. And who'd risk spending a month in the slammer for nicking a Lada! The coppers seemed a jovial crowd, like policemen back home, and when they took me to their firing range I thought it would be a nice gesture to draw them a cartoon target of Lenin. They quickly blasted it to pieces.

Larry ON HOLIDAY

My wife and I regularly receive postcards from friends taking holidays all over the world. By some strange coincidence most of them come from our medical chums – skiing in Colorado having done the Alps too often, or soaking up the sun on some South Pacific island having tired of the Riviera. But I suppose if you're looking at some-one's rotten feet all day or are on 24-hour call as a midwife you've got to get away as much as you can.

For me, of course, cartooning itself is a bit of a holiday. Having been a teacher and a factory-worker and all that I know what real work does to you.

Belting unruly kids and smiling at obnoxious parents, endless marking, clocking in at the works, kowtowing to the boss – in those days if I didn't get away for a few weeks every year I would have gone crackers. But now life's much more civilized.

That said, though, and perhaps so as not to appear odd, my wife and I do sometimes take holidays. Just a motor ride usually, to the Lakes or Cornwall – no hassle with airports and that sort of stuff. And we enjoy the change of scene. But I suppose having

lots of good family fun to be had for the asking. But then of course there was the traditional British weather – lousy. For several years we skipped off in early May–June and had a run of good luck with proper summer sunshine – we got it right so often neighbours even used to time their holidays to coincide with ours as if we were the Chosen People. But then we got overambitious and started booking weeks away at Easter – and drowned. So we don't bother with all that any more.

dogs has something to do with it too – we never like to leave them behind and you can't do that if you go abroad. Poor simple souls that we are, we've even taken other people's dogs with us on holiday to give them a treat !

We no longer bother with the traditional seaside holiday. All those buckets and spades, 'Kiss-me-Quick' hats and coconut shies at the end of the pier. Years ago when the kids were young and small enough to lift onto a donkey without giving me a hernia it seemed a good idea. The best hotels didn't seem to cost a fortune, the beaches were cleaner and there was

READY
KNOTTED
HANDKERCHIEFS

HOMELEA HOTEL

Larry ON DIY

Doing it yourself – whether its putting up shelves, fixing the overflow pipe or painting the windows – has always been more a necessity than an option for the less well off. But I suppose the real DIY boom came in the 1970s when all the cowboy tradesmen were about. Why pay someone to muck up your house when you can wreck it yourself for half the cost!

Decorating is a case in point. In the old days you'd get in a family firm that had been at it man and boy since Boadicea was alive and they'd do a good job, but it would cost you an arm and a leg. And then came the Likely Lads, splashing a tub of Dulux around, whacking on the Polyfilla, bunging in the Rawlpugs with a drill like a tommy-gun whilst next door's cat had a fit, and Bob's your uncle – until it all fell off.

My father was a great DIY fan. His idea of heaven was spending a Saturday morning browsing around the Home Improvements department of Lewis's in Birmingham. He was also a dab hand at wrought-iron work – most of the light fittings in our house in those days were beaten out of strip metal in the garden shed by my old man. When my folks passed on and it came to selling up, I offered to remove all the exotic curled-metal chandeliers and spiral wall lights for the new owners but they were delighted to keep them as they were. I suppose they saw it as 'period style' in the same way as they've recently turned a bungalow in Hall Green, Birmingham, into a museum of 1950s DIY.

It's been many years since I did any DIY, apart from putting up the occasional shelf. But in the 1950s when we bought our first house my wife and I were quite keen on decorating. I suppose it's something that brings couples together, building the nest and all that. This was in the days when emulsion paint and lamb's wool hand-rollers had just been invented so it was a popular pastime, even though the colours did sometimes seem to clash after a week or two and in retrospect the hardware-store man had been right about spending a few extra bob on a water-proof paper for the bathroom. But nowadays, no fear, we get the professionals in. I'm happy to sit next door drawing cartoons to pay their fee and let them get on with it.

A friend of mine once dug himself a pit in his garage so that he could work under his car. Just as he was finishing it off and smoothing down the sides, his wife, who was then in the process of suing him for divorce, deliberately drove the car in and parked it over the pit. He was trapped there for hours before she consented to back it out. Hell hath no fury...

But the best laugh connected with DIY that I can recall was the true story of a man who thought it

would be a good idea to insulate his roof area by pouring Tarmac in the spaces between the joists. After lugging buckets of bitumen up and down stepladders for what seemed an age, he and his wife cleaned up and went to bed. As they settled down contentedly with a well-earned cup of Ovaltine, great cracks began to appear in the ceiling, followed by an avalanche of newly hardened asphalt. They barely escaped with their lives.

Humour and Sickle

In 1983 I was invited to be the UK judge for an International cartoon exhibition at the House of Humour & Satire in Gabrovo, Bulgaria. So I hopped on the Sophia plane at Frankfurt and after a short flight being entertained by stewardesses resembling Elsie Tanner, hopped out again into a time-warp airport that looked like a dog-eared photo of Birmingham circa 1950. I somehow missed the courier sent to page me as he was holding a sign written in Cyrillic, but miraculously managed to find the correct hotel and joined up with the other judges who had winged in from every corner of the globe.

Dinner that evening was memorable for the four-piece band playing Victor Sylvester and the pre-teen dancing couples – children of the management, as local adults couldn't afford to stay there. Equally memorable was the interminable wait for breakfast the following morning while the staff got out of bed, performed their ablutions and served themselves first! This was followed by an invigorating drive along the pot-holed motorway to a reception at Gabrovo Town Hall. Our grand welcoming scene had to be repeated as the BBC crew filming us weren't happy with the first take, and then it was down to the judging at the nearby House of Humour.

I always find massive exhibitions of cartoons rather mind-numbing and this stretched through interminable linked rooms like a show at the Tate Gallery, each drawing individually numbered and categorized by country. When we assembled for the final voting I was completely floored and just gave them random figures based on permutations of my home telephone number – there were some surprised looks but the moment passed. But I wasn't the only one fudging the results – in their efforts to disguise the fact that the East Europeans seemed to be winning everything, the committee invented a new category to accommodate the UK's deficiency in the prize stakes and awarded 100 Livas to Peter Rigby, who – ever the adventurer – promptly blew the lot on entertaining one of the pretty interpreters.

The delights of Gabrovo then awaited us – beautiful Swiss-style mountain ranges offset by abandoned Army trucks, half-built concrete tower-blocks and a sad-looking 'Heritage Park'. But the trip had its high points: some Yanks from National Lampoon stunned the locals in our hotel bar by pretending to inject themselves with drugs using empty syringes . . .

IN SICKNESS AND IN HEALTH

I suppose the older you get the more you think about life, health, illness and death. Mind you, not everybody worries about it – there are some old boys down my local in Stratford who positively relish their decreptitude. As they swill down their ale and tap their dominoes there's no end of one-upmanship about their false teeth, hearing-aids or forthcoming prostate ops. But then again they live to be a good age hereabouts – eighty-five being a fair average. It's spending their lives walking on the flat that does it, I reckon.

Ambulancemen, for me, come pretty

close to firemen in the hero category. I was once in need of their services when I fell off the top of a ladder while pruning a tall tree. It was only a sprained ankle and some dislocated fingers but I got the whole treatment, rushed off to hospital in their little van and everything – though I can't remember the siren going. On another occasion a lad came off his motorbike trying to avoid a neigbour's dog and

landed in our front garden. The boys in grey were soon on the scene to whip him off for treatment – a broken leg and bad concussion. Unfortunately one of them stood on the poor bugger's arm as they lifted him up, but nobody's perfect.

The most recent case of medical drama I was involved in was down a nearby pub. One of the regulars suddenly keeled over at the bar at lunchtime and collapsed in a heap. We all thought he'd had a heart attack and called out the paramedics (a girl and a bloke this time) but by the time they arrived he was as right

44

RODIN
DOCTOR
AND
PATIENT

as rain and looked very sheepish as they carried him out on a stretcher – he'd just drunk one more than his usual ten pints and fainted!

I suppose I like doing drawings about people I admire. I'm not a vindictive cartoonist like some are, and the Health Service workers for me are a breed apart. I once won an award for a series of jokes about Flying Doctors organized by the Italian medical authorities in Verona. They sent me a bronze sculpture of some winged god of medicine or other as a trophy but somehow it got damaged in the post. Anyway, I got a pal to weld it together and it stood on the mantelpiece for a few years, but it seems to have taken flight again recently.

I've also had a lot of friends who've been medics. The trouble is, a lot of them also like going skiing. When we used to live in Solihull, the lounge bar of the George Hotel would look like a casualty ward at the end of March each year as all our pals hobbled in after their holidays – Lord knows who looked after their practices while they were laid up. We non-skiers used to make bets on who would come home with fractures. Top scores were awarded to legs in plaster and broken collar-bones – mere black eyes weren't counted.

Another pal is a dentist. An Aussie, he settled in Walsall but the local Caribbean and Asian community there have very little teeth trouble so he has to rely on rot-jaws like myself. Most of my teeth are capped now and as I insist on smoking a pipe and biting into apples I'm always in and out of his surgery getting them glued back together again. He asked me recently why so few cartoonists do dentist jokes these days. I said I thought it probably had to do with the efficiency of modern technology – having removed the terror, humour can't thrive. But I obliged him by drawing some gags for his walls, basing them on scenes from W. C. Fields's old 1930s' film, *The Dentist*.

WELCOME
BACK
FRED

General healthwise, I suppose I've been lucky so far. I've only been into hospital as a visitor and the only nurses I see regularly are a bunch who tag along on local coach trips from time to time – they always bag the smoking seats at the back, of course, but are good company. On the subject of nurses, my father gave our hospital staff a run for their money in his latter years.

On one occasion he only lasted three days on the ward before he was discharged for bad behaviour – not staying in bed after lights out, arguing with Matron and secret smoking. The final straw was when he was caught in his pyjamas and bare feet running after a confectionery van that sold Woodbines.

Now death is also a subject I take an interest in, especially sitting in the garden puffing my pipe and reading a copy of the *Oldie*. If the magazine asked me, for their 'Death File' column, what would be my ideal way to go I'd say aged 99 flying to Disney World. It would be perfect: the plane would blow up so there wouldn't be any funeral arrangements and I would have been stopped from going somewhere I know I wouldn't have enjoyed!

Undertakers do an important job too, though it's one somewhat lacking in appeal – I don't, for instance, recall it featuring much on the Careers Board at school. But there are people who seem happy to do this kind of work.

I even know of one firm – two men and a lad – who offer a combined service of bricklaying, plumbing, carpentry and undertaking! Which reminds of a story of my father's last moments. As he lay dying in bed, nibbling charcoal biscuits which he'd been prescribed for a severe stomach disorder – he'd eaten nothing else for a month – the district nurse turned up for one of her regular visits. As he watched her coming down the path through the bedroom window he brandished his two hundred and fiftieth charcoal biscuit and said: 'I don't need a nurse to give me an enema – I need a bloody chimney sweep!'

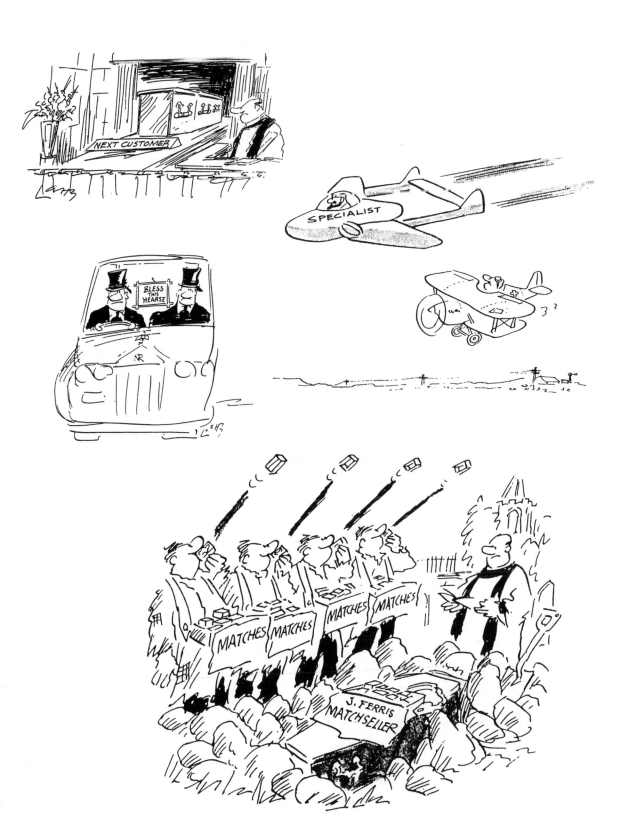

Larry AT CHURCH

I'm not a great churchgoer. The usual rites of passage, I suppose – births, marriages, deaths and all that sort of thing. But I quite like the bells and the singing and the atmosphere, and all those stained-glass windows and stone sculptures. And harvest festivals are good fun for the kids with the fruit displays and the prize marrows, and bits of bread baked like sheaves of wheat, but otherwise I tend to give it a miss.

I've been to a lot of weddings, though. My own went off reasonably well considering, and the photos are trotted out occasionally for a good laugh. The church we were married in stood in a hollow so while the matrimonial team group posed in front of the porch the photographer stood at the top of the hill. The result was that we all appear foreshortened – two families of pigmies in their Sunday best. I also think we went wrong with the hire suits. My best man was considerably slimmer than myself yet his suit is all baggy with concertina trousers while I look as though I've eaten the reception dinner already.

Another wedding I was involved in was when I was driving the groom to the church and we got stuck in a traffic jam behind the bride's car. I had to take off down the sidestreets like Stirling Moss in order to get there first. We arrived with only seconds to spare and just managed to slip in through the vestry door before his beloved reached the altar. And then there was the marriage of one of my son's pals. The groom reckoned he'd been rather shanghaied over the whole affair but put a brave face on it all. The ceremony seemed to drag on a bit but the high point was when they had to kneel down before the crucifix and on the soles of his shoes you could see written the plea 'Help!' (I'd like to be able to say that they're still happily married, but unfortunately they split up after 12 months.)

As per the Royals, about half the people I know are divorcees. The hard-core regulars in my local are now single again (nothing to do with the beer, I'm assured). One of them, the plumber – still working at 72 – got divorced recently after 40 years of marriage. When I suggested it may have had something to do with his habit of carousing till dawn and crawling up the stairs on all fours he stopped me and said: 'No, I divorced *her* – I couldn't stand her looks of contempt.'

There's something rather strange about religion. I never could understand why people with a great deal more intelligence than I have still believe in it – perhaps they've had visions. The only vision I ever had was a recurring nightmare: what if my son should become a vicar? To be fair, I didn't fancy the prospects of his becoming a teacher or a policeman either, but for some illogical reason the idea of him being in the God Squad used to make me break out in a cold sweat and wake up screaming. In the end he became a chartered accountant...

"THE DESCENT FROM THE CROSS"

WEIGHT WATCH-TOWER

JEHOVAH'S SLIMMERS

53

DOWN THE LOCAL

mats for Double Diamond, Newcastle Brown and others, and even produced a huge poster for Tennent's Pilsner with a man on an island surrounded by sharks. But as for beer itself? Well, I was brought up on M&B and am a keen supporter of our local Flowers brew here in Stratford (complete with Shakespeare's head on the label). It's got to be in a jug, of course, with a handle. This straight-glass business is for the slot-machine addict and though I wouldn't call myself an earnest CAMRA man I do sympathize with their aims.

Somehow I seem to have got a reputation for being a beer-swilling Brummie cartoonist and its certainly true that pubs have played a great part in my life. But to be fair I haven't done all that many pub jokes in recent times. Like everybody else I moan about the way they're all being converted into restaurants and the separate rooms knocked into one, and no doubt before long Eurofizz lounges, Space Invader booths, pool parlours, no-smoking areas, coffee corners, children's crèches, dog-kennels and Muzak will be the norm, but it requires a more savage pen than mine to do the subject justice. However, no biography of mine could be an honest one without a pub section and so I include one herewith.

I've done a lot of advertising work for breweries in the past, especially beer

We all have to compromise, though, in this day and age, and the genuine spit-and-sawdust, hand-pump taverns are hard to come by now. In the circumstances I suppose my local is pretty acceptable really: food only at lunchtime, a front bar without music, a token fruit-machine well away from the conversation

area and a clientele aged over 35. There's a back room for the kids to play pool, drink Bacardi and Coke and watch telly. Organized like that everyone's happy, and for those who don't feel comfortable without a dog stretched out in front of the fire there's even a huge St Bernard that keeps the place in order.

A favourite haunt of mine in Birmingham used to be the Woodman in Curzon Street. A well-preserved Victorian pub, it survived the bombing during the war but unfortunately the surrounding area didn't and it now stands isolated amongst warehouses and lorry parks. None the less, it has managed to attract back customers by serving the best traditional pub food in the area – nothing cooked as this would spoil the beer, just hefty doorstep sandwiches and pork pies. When I first went there, with Colin Whittock, Trevor Holder (Holte) and other cartoonist cronies from the *Birmingham Evening Mail*, there was this strange bloke who used to park his lorry outside and always sat in the same place in the lounge. Not surprisingly, he hasn't been in since they locked him up but, perhaps for different reasons, his seat is kept vacant – they've now christened it the Sutcliffe Chair. As one old regular said, they should have known he was a wrong 'un – he always drank lager.

ONE RETIRED BUSINESSMANS'

Cartooning Today

It took a while for the neighbours to figure out what I was up to when I first became a professional cartoonist in 1957. Seeing me padding around in my carpet slippers on a Monday morning – buying cigarettes at the local newsagent at 11 o'clock, walking the dog in daylight, and sitting in an empty pub at lunchtime they assumed I was on sick leave. Then they got it into their heads that I must have become a cat burglar or had switched to night work – in those days everyone seemed to clock in at the office or factory at nine o'clock and working from home gave rise to all sorts of suspicions. Now, of course, there seem to be more people at home than anywhere else – especially cartoonists.

There also seems to be a different attitude these days, In the past cartoonists used to enjoy each other's company – there used to be high jinks down the Sketch Club with Phil May and John Hassall, and my generation would go on boat trips together or take off to Butlins with the Cartoonists' Club. But today's lot seem a morose bunch – about as welcoming as the average traffic warden. I suspect it's because, with the rise in cartoon collecting and the high prices people like Scarfe and Steadman are getting for their pictures, it's all getting a bit too serious.

To my amazement they've even started a postgraduate course in cartooning at the new University of the West Midlands. I know the Principal (he was good enough to make me an Honorary Fellow when it was called the Birmingham Polytechnic) and as he's got a good sense of humour I reckoned at first it must be a leg-pull. But I was wrong – apparently people are enrolling like mad. I can't understand it, you can't teach how to be a cartoonist – or a stand-up comedian for that matter– you're either funny or you aren't. But maybe I'm being unfair. You can certainly teach drawing style if not humour. In the past most of us started by cribbing from each other's styles – Giles, Thelwell and Searle were probably the most influential when I started out – and perhaps that's what they'll be doing at UWM, copying others until their own style comes through. There's a lot of similarity in published work these days, sometimes only apparently differing in the signature – imitators of Larson, Glen Baxter, Mike Heath and the other successful artists abound, and to be a syndicated political cartoonist in the USA you won't get a look in unless you draw exactly like Oliphant. But the more I think about it I suppose it was ever thus – in the 1930s lots of cartoonists' stuff looked exactly like Low's, and in more recent times the influence of Giles on JAK and MAC can't be denied.

One thing the modern school don't seem to do, though – probably because they don't mix so much with their contemporaries – is to include each other's names in the cartoons themselves. People like Martin Honeysett, Clive Collins, Chic Jacob, Bill Tidy and myself have always put each other's names on cartoon noticeboards or used them as characters. A good example was in Ken Pyne's cartoon novel, Martin Minton. In a queue for the Labour Exchange Martin discovers his school careers master, Mr Parkes, behind him. It's a double joke for me, of course – not only did I used to be a schoolteacher, but in the early days of Ken's career I used to coach him a bit with his cartooning. Don't ask me why I bothered.

Larry ON CHRISTMAS

Christmas has come round for me so often it's got to be a bit of a bore. Miserable buggers, my wife and I. We've made a decision never again to pin up Christmas cards or decorations. No more Christmas trees, no bloody fairy-lights that fuse, and no crackers that go phut and dispense plastic rings and paper hats that don't fit. As for the religious side, that passes me by altogether – I'd as soon celebrate Confucius's birthday. New Year's is more the ticket – for us it's a sort of celebration of getting past Christmas!

None the less, we cartoonists are forced to face up to the Festive Season when Christmas-card design commissions come flooding in. Even the most sophisticated companies seem to want a

jovial Santa on their cards and sometimes a red-nosed reindeer or two as well – last year I found myself drawing four of them sitting around a table playing cards (or was it Monopoly?).

Christmas seemed to be OK in the old days. I rarely had much to drink then, smoking wasn't frowned upon and we used to play parlour games. I could remain cheerful and not argumentative all through Christmas Day and Boxing Day. We even listened to the Queen's Speech. But now it's all different. And worst of all are the specially written Christmas pop songs – although I quite liked the heavy-metal version of 'Silent Night' . . .

Our kids loved Christmas when my father was alive. They'd always look forward to his visit and beg him to make his famous funny face. So, year after year, out would come his false teeth, on would go the rubber bands and there'd be whoops of laughter as he transformed himself into the most grotesque gargoyle imaginable. Once he even stuck a cobnut up each nostril and played King Kong, chasing them shrieking all over the house. There was a moment's panic later when he had a job prising the nuts out again!

In more recent times we've tended to stay in hotels over the Yuletide period, generally somewhere we've had a good time in the summer holidays. One year in the 1970s we unwittingly missed out on a good beano. We'd been invited to a hotel in Lynton, Devon (only select guests were asked by the proprietor as they didn't want all and sundry turning up – after all, it was their Christmas too). Anyway, winter started early that year with a vengeance and the snow was coming down like it was a new Ice Age. In such arctic conditions we didn't fancy tackling the treacherous Porlock Hill approach road so decided to give it a miss. We were right, of course, and the hotel became totally snowbound and cut off from civilization.

What we didn't know, till we got a card showing them snowballing on the roof, was that as a result the trapped guests ate and drank completely free for ten days until relief arrived.

The real horror for me at Christmas is shopping for presents. The rest of the year my wife does all the shopping – she even buys my clothes. Choosing presents is, for me, near torture. It's not so much the money as the ideas – my wife's dressing-table has drawers stuffed solid with unworn leather gloves and watches. I just don't seem to be able to think of anything original. People say giving books is always fairly safe, but I find it just as difficult as deciding on the right tie. You can always find some use for them, though – and in case any unfortunate types have been given this dog-eared collection for a present I suggest it is handed over immediately to the nearest group of children under seven for colouring in.

Cartoonists of Yesteryear

*I remember in the 1930s seeing huge cartoon advertising posters by John Hassall,
Harry Rountree and the like, and the bookshops and libraries seemed to be packed
with volumes of cracking drawings by H.M.Bateman, Bert Thomas, Bruce
Bairnsfather (creator of 'Old Bill') and others. Then, of course, papers like the*
Daily Mirror *were publishing strips such as 'Just Jake' and 'Ruggles' whilst
classic kids comics like* Chips *and* Film Fun *kept the youngsters laughing with
superb drawings.*

*One or two of yesterday's giant cartoonists are still with us, of course – David
Langdon and the great Carl Giles for a start. I used to dote on Giles's stuff during
the war years. But perhaps the ones that have influenced me most have been
the old* Punch *cartoonists, particularly those who joined just before the war.
People like Lawrie Siggs and John Taylor always used to make me smile as I sat
in line at the barber's shop waiting for my short back and sides. Emett's amazing
drawings fascinated me but never made me laugh – and somehow I seem to have
missed out on Pont altogether. I expect his humour was a bit too sophisticated
for a ten-year old. Osbert Lancaster's stuff I loved, especially his architectural books
(which are very useful if you ever need a crib for a building style . . . .) But if I was
asked to choose my all-time favourite cartoonist it would have to be Starke. No
hesitation about it – Heath Robinson, Bateman, Hoffnung were all dazzling artists
but to me they were never as amusing as Les Starke at his best.*

LARRY ON SPORT

Most cartoonists I know of aren't great sporting buffs and rarely if ever give the subject much time except once every four years when the Olympics are on. And sport in general seems to have got a bit distasteful recently: all that punching in the air after scoring a goal in soccer; McEnroe yelling abuse at tennis umpires; 'sledging' at the wicket in cricket. Not to mention all those unshaven captains...

Never mind, cricket is always good for a laugh. Latest score: England all out for zero. One of the best laughs of recent times was the discovery that most of the paintings in the Lords Taverners' toilet are fakes. Cricket was a good subject for cartoons when Bernard Hollowood was Editor of *Punch* in the '50s and '60s. He'd been a minor-league player with Staffordshire in his youth so was keen on the game, and I suppose the typical *Punch* readership must have included rugby-playing doctors, tennis-playing lawyers, cricketing accountants and the like. But after Hollowood's time sport took a back seat in the magazine.

I expect golfing dentists also read *Punch* but somehow golf has never sunk its hooks into me as it has into so many of my generation. I don't know why. Perhaps it's because I don't want to make my wife a golf widow. It's not that I've not had the opportunity, mind you. I've got an old uncle who used to be a golf professional and I used to caddy for him when I was a teenager. A good friend of mine – not much younger than myself – is an all-round sportsman and played cricket and rugger until quite recently and still plays tennis and squash, but not golf. Why not golf, I asked him one day. 'Because I can't stand the people who play it – all bloody fascists,' he replied. Well, that's as maybe. But I'm not averse to thinking up golf jokes. You can always guarantee to sell originals on this subject – Christmas presents from wives to husbands and so forth.

RODIN'S IRISH JUDGE

The only pity is that the ground was so intensively mined in the 1930s – it's impossible to outshine the likes of H.M.Bateman and Frank Reynolds.

I wasted my time playing soccer as a lad. Anyone with an ounce of sense could have seen that I was custom-built to be a prop forward, but we didn't play rugger at our school. When I was doing my teacher-training practice I found myself put down for a Staff v. Boys rugby match but shamefacedly had to confess I'd never played the game. I'll never forget the look of contempt our pint-sized captain gave me as he crossed his best 'heavy' off the list.

Apart from the anglers whose concentration Gerda disturbs when she swan-dives into the water, the only other sports people I tend to encounter regularly on my walks along the Avon are joggers, rowing types and cyclists. Which reminds me – the only cartoonist I know who was also a serious sportsman is Frank Dickens, creator of the 'Bristow' strip. Apparently he was so good a cyclist in his youth that he nearly made it into the British team for the Rome Olympics. I've never seen Frank actually cycling but somehow he reminds me a bit of the French comedian Jacques Tati and I can't help thinking that he'd probably ride rather like the postman in *Jour de Fêtes*. One new sport that's a natural for cartoonists to draw these days is bunjee-jumping. In fact most of us would probably like to encourage certain editors to take up this pastime – so long as we can be in charge of the length of the rope. Splat!

I've done quite a few gags on the Armed Forces, mostly on the Army and Navy – some of my earliest drawings for *Punch* involved sailors, usually turning on some problem with parrots, wooden legs or visits to brothels. The RAF jokes have been a bit thin on the ground over the years, though – I suppose I've tended to leave the Brylcreem boys to people like Russell Brockbank, David Langdon and those of the officer-and-gentleman class of cartoonists who have specialized in this field.

My only practical Senior Service experience consisted of two trips on aircraft-carriers. Ex-matelot cartoonist Tugg Wilson, who seemed to have pals who were admirals, managed to wangle a group of us onto HMS *Invincible* (doing trials in the Solent) and HMS *Hermes*, arriving by helicopter in the latter case. On the *Invincible* our party of ageing cartoonists – including Bill Tidy, Chic

Jacob and Nick Baker – were hosted by the ship's doctor. Apart from being the only crew member of our age group he was also the only one with any free time, as the sole occupant of the sick bay was a flu case. It turned out that though a naval surgeon commander he had spent his entire career as a landlubber and this was his first time at sea. After the trials the ship was due to sail to California and the voyage was to be his retirement present. Unfortunately, shortly after our weekend aboard, the Falklands War broke out and *Invincible* sailed off to battle in the South Pacific – some retirement present!

Now the Army, of course, I can draw from personal experience in the gunners during my National Service – plenty of material here from sergeant-majors to spud-bashing. It was during my period in the Army that I met people born outside Birmingham for the first time in my life, learnt how to

spend a whole week's earnings in one evening at the NAAFI (only cissies had anything left to spend 24 hours after pay-parade) and had my eyes opened to the vagaries of female choice when matters of service rank are involved. I also learnt to swear and can remember coming home on leave and asking my rather genteel mother at tea-time to pass the effing jam. But as I rarely put words in my cartoons this aspect of Forces humour has never featured very prominently in my drawings.

One particular line I did develop for a time was Royal Signals display cyclists – the White Helmets. Apparently they've got a long history that goes back to the 1930s when they performed without the distinctive skidlids and I suppose must have been called something else. But my memory of them is at country fêtes, piled up in pyramids on their motor-bikes like an Italian circus act, with the vicar's dog yapping like fury and everyone's Mum biting their nails to the quick with worry. They've got a sort of monopoly on this act. It's perhaps not so dangerous as wing-walking or flying with the Red Arrows but nevertheless I think the guy who has to make the top of the triangle must have pretty strong nerves. I've yet to see them come a cropper in a display even though it usually rains and they have to work in appalling conditions. Grand chaps they are - the only act worth coming out of the beer tent to watch.

Comedians

*One of the biggest influences on me from the earliest days were Laurel and Hardy.
We used to watch them at Saturday-morning film shows when I was a kid and I am
pleased to see that through TV and video a whole new generation still finds them
funny – in fact one of my fondest memories was watching the faces of my son and
daughter when they were young and a Laurel and Hardy movie was on the box.*

*Later I discovered the Marx Brothers, W.C.Fields, Will Hay and more recently
Jacques Tati. But the one British comedian I've always felt should have been
up there with the gods was Sid Field. He only made two films,* London Town *and*
Cardboard Cavalier, *neither of which was much cop really, but when he played
pantos in his home town of Birmingham or in London's Piccadilly Theatre nobody
could touch him. Bob Hope was one of his biggest fans.*

*Modern-day comedians I find a bit of a mixed bunch, though I quite like Smith
and Jones, Robbie Coltrane and Ruby Wax – and Harry Enfield is always good for a
belly laugh. But none the less, I've watched* Monsieur Hulot's Holiday *nine times
now and Laurel and Hardy films till I know every word, and somehow I don't relate
in the same way to the modern 'surreal' stuff – not even the Goons or Monty Python.
That Sid Field really had something for me, and my Dad was so keen on him that
he even owned one of his cast-off suits!*

ITALIAN PRISONERS OF WAR
F. S. LOWRY

IMPERIAL WAR MUSEUM

Larry ON PETS

*W*ay back in the 1950s and '60s when humour was gentler and 'satire' was a word only applied to Jonathan Swift and Voltaire, you could sell jokes about pet-owning. I've done dogs, cats, tortoises, goldfish – whatever, and then for some reason I got stuck on budgerigars. I don't know why – I've never owned one myself as there's always been a pair of cats in our household (we did risk buying a hamster for our son once, aged six, but the Siamese finished him off within a month).

My father had a blue budgie – Billy was his name. He would spend all day on his own, mighty depressed until my Dad returned home from work and took him out of his cage to play football with a table-tennis ball. My folks at that time lived in a bungalow with no central heating and during the winter months the poor bird would be frozen rigid on his perch. To bring him round my father used to fill a thimble with gin and the little chap would drink it up and feel great. He died of cirrhosis of the liver aged eight.

Our favourite pets, though, have always been dogs, and my wife and I can be perfect bores in the company of dogless types. Unfortunately, there are an increasing number of them these days – we are no longer a nation of dog-lovers, it seems. 'No Dogs' signs proliferate in pubs and hotels, on beaches, and even in

down a bit. We own a huge Rottweiler bitch who, despite the media image, is as gentle as a kitten. She never fights other dogs and if the odd mutt has the temerity to bite her backside she just gives it a withering look and walks on. Unfortunately, she has the unusual habit of growling with pleasure which can put some people off. You stroke Gerda and she growls like a cat purrs. They are basically very sensible dogs, bark very little and are bone idle – which suits me these days. We used to have a loveable

some public parks. I blame it on the 'health fascists' as Auberon Waugh calls them. It's different in France. The last time I was in Boulogne we were sitting in a café with a bunch of Brits when a dog came begging at the table. One of the lads who hated dogs gave it a boot and we thought nothing more of it. The next day we went to the same place for a coffee and found ourselves barred – it turned out he'd kicked the owner's pet.

I am afraid that the Rottweiler jokes, that I have done have let the side

Labrador that lived to the age of 16. At the age of ten she decided she didn't really like walking and preferred swimming, so when we moved to Stratford I used to stroll along the banks of the Avon as she ploughed through the anglers' lines. We met a lot of people that way, not all of them very happy, though. A lovely dog she was, but she expected you to give her fun all the time: fetch the stick, running about and all-in wrestling. You don't have to do that with Gerda – and I particularly wouldn't recommend the wrestling.

Larry ON LAW AND ORDER

*W*e've never had much to do with the police. Apart from the odd speeding ticket and parking fine, of course. We tend to keep our noses clean and stick to the straight and narrow where possible. No filching from Sainsbury's or smuggling fags through customs – I've not even been done for drunk and disorderly (must be my abstemious habits!).

There have been the usual civil encounters, of course – the young officer who rescued a neigbour's cat from our roof, the one who held up the traffic at our wedding so that the guests could cross the road to the reception at the hotel opposite, and once I even found myself inside Scotland Yard itself. This was at the invitation of a future chief constable then in charge of public relations. The kindly face of the Force, he looked more like a university don than your ''Ello, 'ello, 'ello' stereotype Plod. As we chatted over lunch at the Yard I had the brass-knuckle to ask him why he did it, why the hell he'd become a copper. He seemed a bit vague, I recall – something to do with absent-mindedly attending an interview with the Met when he was at college and they were so welcoming it would have been rude to refuse. And the more of his colleagues I bumped into the more I could see what he meant. They seemed an agreeable lot and later, swapping pints in the canteen, I almost felt like I was one of them – an uncanny sensation.

Now as far as prisons go I can't claim much experience at all. I did have an Army pal when we were stationed in Newport whose uncle was locked up in Parkhurst nick. It always used to amaze me how much better the

conditions were inside the clink than we had back at the camp – maybe it's not surprising that they later converted the barracks itself into a prison!

On one occasion I found myself in the company of no less than three ex-cons. This was when an engineering company commissioned me to draw some cartoons on the difficulties their drivers encountered overseas, especially the problems they had with Customs. So I flew out to Frankfurt and met these three burly drivers and their mammoth Volvo trucks who were about to set off back home loaded to the gunnels with printing presses. They'd parked them in a factory yard in Offenbach, blocking the exit, and at knocking-off time were surrounded by an angry crowd of German workers screaming abuse at them. The truckers never turned a hair - they were brewing-up on a Primus and eating their sandwiches and weren't going to move until they were good and ready. I knew then that I was with a tough bunch.

I only learnt they were ex-cons as we drove back. One had done two years for half-murdering a nightclub bouncer, the second had been sent down for

'hoisting' (he was a professional shoplifter), but the third was less forthcoming – probably a rapist was my guess. For all that, though, they were good company. We cruised through a few bars between Offenbach and Dover but, to my surprise, they were very conscientious about their drinking – two pints each at the most with eight-hour intervals in between.

Another aspect of the law-and-order business is court life. Once I accompanied a magistrate pal to Worcester Crown Court where he was assisting a judge at the trial of a young drugs offender. After a particularly long harangue between the opposing

lawyers the judge ordered an adjournment. Watching from the gallery I could see my friend and the judge go off for a while and then reappear looking considerably more relaxed. Afterwards I quizzed my friend over what particular detail of the case had brought about the adjournment. 'Oh it was nothing to do with the case,' he said. 'The judge just wanted a smoke.'

The Royals

The only Royal I've ever met was Prince Charles back in 1978. It was at the Press Club for the launch of the cartoon anthology, We Are Amused. *After queuing to be frisked for concealed weapons, Semtex, Republican flags and the like, various Fleet Street hacks and contributing artists were ushered into a room hung on all sides with cartoons about royalty, from Gillray to Trog. I was surprised to find myself represented in the show as I couldn't recall having done much on the subject of Their Highnesses – except a few on Charles at Timbertop as a lad – but there I was.*

A path had been roped off along the walls displaying the drawings and guests were supposed to congregate in the middle of the room while the Prince shuffled along the gangway pretending to admire our work. However, he arrived late and so eager were some of the milling throng to catch a glimpse of the Heir Apparent that they broke ranks and mobbed him, leaning over the ropes and proffering hands of welcome. Somewhat disillusioned by our fellows, three of us decided to abandon the scene and adjourned to the bar. After a period of comparative peace staring into our beer-mugs, who should appear through the swing doors but HRH himself – accompanied by a single escort – looking for a quiet pint and the Visitors Book, which he dutifully signed. As a result Ken Pyne, Martin Honeysett and yours truly had him to ourselves for the best part of ten minutes. He was charming enough, even though he confessed to being a fan of Ken Pyne's and admitted to having some of his drawings hanging in the Royal Loo. Oh well, there's no accounting for taste!

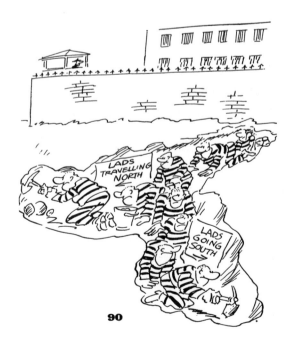

LARRY ON THE WORKERS

*D*uring the bad old days of the Labour Government when there was full employment and everyone had a job (when they weren't striking), there was, ironically, a shortage of skilled workers on the domestic scene. All the plumbers, chippies and brickies were taken up with building new office blocks and high-rise flats and had no time for private household work. As a result the field was open for a new breed of cowboy.

Nowadays it's not too difficult to find a reliable tradesman. Poke your head in our local and whistle and unemployed skilled workers will drop their pints and rush to do your bidding. But in the 1970s you had to grab who you could and often this meant some spotty-faced 15-year-old straight out of school. Flung in at the deep end it's not surprising they botched the work: 'Here, son, build me a garage', 'Oh, you've never done a loft conversion before? Well, now's the time to try.' Alan Coren, *Punch* Editor at the time, must have been a victim of one of these types because in a rare phone call he asked me to draw a page about cowboy plumbers. It was an instant success and from then on there was no stopping me – brickies, scaffolders, construction-workers and others quickly followed.

Of course, I've done other cartoons about tradesmen who put in a lot of honest graft – butchers, milkmen, postmen and the like. Indeed some of my best pals have been small family butchers, but a lot of them are going out of business in the recession.

Then, of course, there are the factory-workers, and having spent some time in factories myself I think I usually get the humour about right – blokes swinging

the lead, playing darts or cards behind packing-cases, works canteen gags, things going wrong on the conveyor belt etc. I even did a whole book of 'Man in Factory' jokes.

motor industry in recent years has been adverts for Esso Superlube oils.

Come to think of it, advertising jobs have often led me to draw cartoons about workers, and in the course of business I've been on guided tours of chocolate factories, whisky distilleries, breweries, plastics and rubber companies, glassmakers and drug manufacturers. I've even been doing some jokes recently for a local firm that makes

And coming from the Midlands I particularly like doing drawings about car-workers. When we lived in Solihull we were surrounded by them. Not only that but many of my relatives worked in the car trade for Austin, Wolseley, Riley and BSA motorbikes. In those days, of course, there were panellers, welders, tool-fitters and jigborers but now its all automated so there's less interest in it from a cartoonist's point of view. In fact the nearest I've got to the

agricultural machinery. I'm quite fond of the hedgerow-cutters but my favourite is the machine that turns all the hay into neat, tightly packed cylindrical bales. If he were alive today John Constable would have hated the fields of bright yellow rape-seed but I'm sure he would have loved these. The only trouble is that they would probably have rolled off his famous haywain and into the pond at Flatford Mill!

My Studio

Years ago I used to work from home but my wife found that I cluttered the place up too much, so as soon as we could afford it I rented an office in Birmingham town centre to keep out of her way. Since we've been in Stratford I've been using a flat on the opposite side of town to our house. It's quiet and convenient (only 100 yards from the Slug and Lettuce, should inspiration flag), has a kitchen, bathroom, bedroom and all mod cons and, as studios go – though I've never called it that – fits the bill perfectly.

My working methods are simple. Sitting in an easy chair I usually light my pipe (I usually buy reject ones – why spend lots of money on something you can't try out in the shop?), pull out some fresh A4 Croxley Script or the backs of some old discarded drawings and doodle away until I've got a few ideas I'm happy with. I then work them up, but always on paper small enough to fit easily into a letterbox (a tip I got from the late Leslie Starke). For the finished drawings I use a mapping pen with nibs they stopped making years ago – I've only got a dozen left so when they're bent beyond repair I'll probably retire – and Pelikan ink. Brushes, though elegant, I find too slow and as a guide you generally have to do a pencil line first whereas I prefer to draw straight onto the paper in ink. And much though I love a very soft pencil I'd have to keep a full-time assistant to sharpen up the 8B points, so I tend to give them a miss too. Felt-tip pens I could never get on with as the ink fades too fast – who wants to buy a cartoon that becomes invisible after two years? For colour work I usually use coloured inks as I find watercolours have a habit of obscuring the lines. Greetings card companies are particularly keen on bright primary colours, but I'm not, which is probably why I don't do many. I always say that it is the old black-and-white designs by artists like E.H.Shepard which stand out in shops these days – but will they listen?

Unlike David Low and the great cartoonists of the past I don't work at a sloping drawing-board but sit huddled over my desk surrounded by mucky pots and half-empty coffee mugs. Behind me the wall is covered with racks of categorized photographic references for detail work and to my left is a window looking out over a secluded sidestreet. The other two walls are covered with bits and bobs: cartoons by friends, early art-school daubs in long-forgotten styles (signed 'T.Parkes'), paintings by my father (an accomplished 'primitive'), photos of the family and pets, portraits by my daughter (trained at the Slade), various bits of memorabilia from jobs and foreign trips, and hanging on the back of the door my trusty cloth cap – never washed and still showing the teeth marks from our dear old Labrador. And for those who are interested in whose cartoons I've got in my loo, all can now be revealed – above the poster of Lenin (a souvenir from my Kiev trip) hang two Ken Pyne originals (best place for them, I reckon).

I wouldn't say I was a great music fan and I certainly have 'mixed feelings', as they say, about some of the contemporary stuff, both classical and pop. But I like the old standards – things you can hum along to or sing in the bath, if you can remember the words.

I've got an uncle who is very musical. At the age of 13 he was playing the piano accompaniment to silent films at the local fleapit and by all accounts spent the whole of World War II tickling the ivories in RAF officers' messes the length and breadth of India. After he was demobbed he played in orchestras and broadcast regularly on BBC radio but found work started to dry up with the coming of the pop scene and switched to insurance. Now retired, he lives in a sound-proofed house filled with the latest recording equipment, a grand piano and an enormous organ. We always love to

go round to hear him play Bach's Toccata and Fugue and watch his 80-year-old legs whizzing up and down like pistons.

In recent years I must confess I've also rather taken to opera. A strange hobby for a working-class Brummie you might feel and, to be fair, I used to need a lot of persuading to take the fat ladies and their glass-shattering arias seriously (my wife's the real opera buff) but of late I've come right round to it. Living in Stratford,

of course, theatre is obviously more readily available than opera but we do get the touring companies – the Welsh and Opera North – and despite my earlier misgivings I'm now quite a fan. I've even been doing some cartoons for *Opera Now* and find that it lends itself to even more humour than 'straight' theatre.

I've been a serious student of the off-duty 'straight' actor at the bar of the Dirty Duck and the Arden Hotel in Stratford for some years now. On the whole they're a self-contained

when they got to the feast scene towards the end, the sight of all those cooked chickens, ducks and pheasants and huge baskets of fruit made me nearly leap on stage. They were all wax, of course, but it seemed to me that I wasn't the only one whose eyes were out on stalks. This was just before the Iron Curtain fell and the Kiev audience hadn't seen decent food like this for many a long year.

Stratford has a very high standard of buskers – string quartets, visiting American horn-players, solo flautists and so on. Best of all in my view are the West Indian steel bands which sound so good in the open air and seem to be playing classics all of their own. But you never see any pop musicians, no folkies with a finger stuck in one ear or blues guitarists singing about their doggone bad-luck souls – the stalwart burghers of Stratford don't want to listen to that sort of thing, the police have instructions to move them on.

bunch, only interested in themselves. It was the same when I was painting backdrops for Joan Littlewood's Theatre Workshop. But the opera gang are a completely different kettle of fish – they seem much jollier and a lot more outgoing. I was even able to treat an Opera North Don Giovanni to a pint recently and we had a good old natter.

There was one opera I really didn't enjoy, though, and that was a performance of *Don Giovanni* in Ukranian. It wasn't the language that was the problem – I was in Kiev at the time with a party from Central TV who were the guests of the local station, Gostel TV – but we'd only landed a couple of hours before and were jet-lagged and tired. Not only was keeping awake a serious problem but like most of us I was also starving, having missed my Sunday roast. So

Buyers and Sellers

It's always a surprise to us cartoonists to find that people actually want to buy the original. Mind you, I've picked up the odd Phil May, Frank Reynolds or Lewis Baumer myself – and examples of most of my mates' work are dotted around the flat where I do most of my drawing – but I got those for different reasons. Occasionally in the old days people used to write in to the paper or magazines to ask for the original of something that had been printed but nothing like the way dealers and collectors do today. In many ways I've been lucky in this respect. The very first cartoon I had published in Punch *– of a horse-owner talking to a jockey while studying him through binoculars – was bought up by the trainer Major Dennison, but there was a long gap after that before I sold any more.*

Robin Ray and Bernard Levin set up a gallery in London to sell cartoons in the late 1960s but it didn't pay its way and eventually closed. And then along came Mel Calman who somehow got the balance right with his The Workshop (now The Cartoon Gallery) and is still trading today after more than 20 years. Of the newer arrivals on the scene credit must go to Chris Beetles, operating in Ryder Street, St James's, who as well as the work of classic book illustrators from the past has recently been including joke cartoonists such as myself. In his opinion contemporary cartoonists are hugely underrated and the prices for their work are far too low. I'll drink to that, Mr B.

Larry ON FIREMEN

Up to date I've never had my house set on fire. My wife swears it's bound to happen one day the way I leave my smouldering pipe lying all over the shop. Singed carpets we've had but so far no real conflagration.

Mind you, I've witnessed a few good fires in my time. The first memory I have is during the Blitz in Birmingham. My uncle was in the National Fire Service and I remember watching his team one Sunday morning as they played their hoses amongst the smouldering ruins of a furniture store in Smallbrook Street that had been devastated by a bombing raid the previous night. By the time we got there the worst was over and a lot of the furniture had been saved by dragging it out of the building. When I looked round for my uncle I spotted him taking his ease on one of the posh sofas in the middle of the street!

I can also remember incendiaries dropping into the gardens in our neighbourhood – one even landed in next door's coal-shed and a year's supply went up in smoke. Later, when I was 15, I went off to London for the first time and stayed in the YHA hostel in Highgate. A huge fire started in a nearby tyre depot and, after trips to the Tower, Madame Tussaud's and the National Gallery earlier that day, rounded off my visit with a superb night's entertainment.

The last good fire I watched was at a local greengrocer's shop. The owners, who we knew, looked pretty fed up as they saw their business disappearing in flames, but not so their three kids – all under nine.

Whooping with joy and excitement they hopped in and out of the sweating firefighters, getting in their way and creating chaos amongst the water-jets and crackling timber.

I rate firemen very highly – with

be involved with the show at one time and she was looking for new ideas. 'What about "Birmingham's Burning",' I suggested, but it didn't seem to fit the bill somehow...

In the early 1970s I met a lot of firemen once in the course of business. This was when I was painting cartoon scenery for Joan Littlewood's Theatre Workshop. They'd somehow managed to dragoon a whole gang of off-duty firemen into helping with the props and so I had teams of them hopping up ladders to fill in the colours on the topmost parts of the big panels. Ideally we would have laid them out horizontally but the corridors were too narrow and there

ambulancemen they are real heroes in my eyes. It's a dangerous job and I suppose that's what makes TV programmes like 'London's Burning' such compulsive viewing for couch potatoes like me. We've got a neighbour who used to

wasn't much space so they had to go upright. We were using aniline dyes so there wasn't too much trouble with it running. The only problem was that we mixed the paint up in pint glasses from the bar and as we were also being regularly supplied with beer from the same source there would be the occasional mix-up. But the firemen took it all in good heart. As one of them said, it didn't taste much different - it was only Ben Truman.

Larry ON ART

Art in St Margaret's Primary School, Handsworth, was a poor affair – plant-drawing and painting in watercolour. The teacher would say things like 'Next Monday everybody must bring a daffodil to paint.' Come the day we would set to and start fencing with the daffs until they'd end up very sad-looking in their jam-jars. We were once asked to draw a set of step-ladders as a test of perspective – it was a swine but I enjoyed it.

At grammar school, where art was a bit of a Cinderella subject, we had a good teacher called Lulu (his real name was Mr Llewellyn) and he was a great fan of poster art. This was during the war years when Ashley Cooper and Abraham Games were at their peak and so we did views through U-boat periscopes, 'Careless Talk Cost Lives' or, for the still-life group, 'Grow More Vegetables'. Being a bit of a show-off (only in the art class, mind), when it came to sitting the art tests for School Certificate, I finished off the drawings for a couple of others as well as my own. But as they say, pride always comes before a fall – when the results were published they both got distinctions and I only got a pass!

Art school was a good time for me and I particularly liked the Life Class. On one memorable occasion in the depths of winter – it must have been around 1944/5 – a huge icicle formed on a chimney and hung down directly over the glass dome covering the main stairwell. Two of us thought it would be a great wheeze to take it down and stick it on the model's throne and watch it melt. So we got up onto the roof and started dislodging the icicle – which must have been all of 12 feet long with a base of about 2 feet. Of course, we should have known that it would weigh about the same as a family car – it slid through our fingers, plummeted through the glass dome and zoomed down six floors like a doodlebug, hurling broken glass and ice into the sculpture rooms and caretaker's office. Thinking it really was a bomb, everyone rushed

MILLAIS

CUBIST PERIOD

into the air-raid drill and the place was bedlam. My mate and I scarpered and hid out in the Gaumont Cinema until the panic subsided. However, though our absence drew suspicion, we never got caught.

The staff themselves were capable of pranks, too. As a result of police inquiries after an incident one day it was discovered that the assistant head of the sculpture department had been firing hard clay balls from a cannon at adjoining offices and had even reached the Birmingham Council building!

I got my art teacher's diploma and then it was three years teaching before becoming a professional cartoonist. However, I very nearly got into 'serious' art as an illustrator. I used to fancy myself as the new Ardizzone, Spurrier, Minton or Bawden (another reason for signing my cartoons 'Larry', saving my real name for the proper stuff), and James Boswell, Art Editor of *Lilliput* magazine, took a fancy to my portfolio. But he only published a few cartoons and the posh commissions never materialized before the magazine was axed.

The real giant for me, however – even though he was only four foot tall – has to be Toulouse-Lautrec. Seeing his work at the Hayward in 1991 really brought it home to me that he was up there with the greatest of the great. In fact I've put together a football team of the artists I think are the real

The 'A' Team

VELAZQUEZ CEZANNE MONET TITIAN MUNCH

RENOIR CHARDIN

TOULOUSE-LAUTREC VERMEER REMBRANDT DEGAS MANET

VINCENT

RODIN'S
SOFT
PORNOGRAPHER

collection, this time for David & Charles Ltd, and then came the offer for an exhibition at the Walker Art Gallery, Liverpool (they'd just done Bill Tidy), followed by the Chris Beetles Gallery in London. So it seems to have caught on – long may it continue. The Rodin sculpture jokes don't really belong in the art section – there's no need to be an art-gallery fan to get the gist – so I've spread them around the book under the various headings. When I started doing them I wasn't particularly inter-ested in his work – I just needed a vehicle for some gags that needed captions. Elizabeth Frink was more my cup of tea. But when I read she admired him I looked at his stuff with a fresh eye and was tempted to draw his style more accurately – he didn't do big noses and his muscles were usually in the right places. I soon real-ized that would be fatal, so I quickly reverted to my usual balls-up-first-go technique – and it seems to work out OK.

champions. The 11 regulars are Rembrandt (captain), Van Gogh (centre forward), Velàzquez, Manet, Monet, Degas, Lautrec, Vermeer, Chardin, Brueghel and Turner, though there are occasional substitutions from the bench.

On the cartoon side my early influences were Carl Giles, Les Starke, the French artist Bosc – I probably got the big-nose style from him – and Ludwig Bemelmans. My quirky line stems directly from art school – one of my teachers, a Mr Gledhill, showed me how to bear down on the pencil for emphasis, 'leave lighter drawn lines to suggest, rather than spell out'. Since then I've always driven the blockmakers crazy.

Doing gags about art began when Tony Rushton – Art Editor of *Private Eye* and himself a former art-school student (Royal College) – fancied plunging into book publishing. The result was *Larry's Art Collection*. It was well received but didn't sell in large numbers. Then I did another

TABLE PLAN

FRIENDS OF THE ROYAL ACADEMY ANNUAL DINNER

113

Larry ON THE ROAD

*F*or me it used to be hell owning a motor car. Not being in the least bit mechanical, a breakdown in the middle of nowhere – or even in the middle of somewhere – used to send me into a panic. Not that I'm a particularly panicky person, but having my car stop suddenly for no good reason in the centre of London, say, was catastrophic.

I tried BMWs in the 1970s in an attempt to buy something known for its reliability. These went wrong on me far more often than the Fords I had driven before. Even the second-hand Jag I

once owned had done better. In fact, if I were to draw up a league table of all the cars I have possessed since 1957, the BMWs would rank bottom for reliability. The first one I owned I kept ten years – an expensive mistake. It finally seized up with a cracked cylinder head and I sold it to a Sikh. He struck a tough bargain as the upholstery was a mass of dog hairs, but I was glad to be rid of the heap. Strolling past the Birmingham Law Courts some months later I was amazed to see it on the road again,

resprayed fire-engine red, covered in badges and fitted with a carphone. I congratulated the new owners – a smartly dressed West Indian couple - on the appearance of the old car and they gave me a strange look. It never occurred to me till later that perhaps someone had just switched the plates...

We decided to give up on BMWs altogether when my wife spotted a brand-new Honda sitting on the forecourt of a recently opened garage

116

one day. Smashing little thing it was. Automatic, of course – I can't stand all that shunting about with gears. We fell for it on the spot and it proved a gem, as has every subsequent Jap car we've bought. We currently own a Subaru Estate Turbo as I like getting a move on down motorways – it's a lot safer than tootling around in the slow lane with huge Juggernauts breathing down your neck – and the station-wagon version caters well for the dogs and odd bits of antique furniture that have to be shifted around with my wife's business.

I wouldn't say I was a car-nutter but it's probably true to say that I can recognize most models these days from practically any angle. This is all the result of

constant dog-walking – to relieve the boredom I study parked cars in Stratford, mentally calculating the number of foreign versus UK makes. But I don't count anything younger than E-registration. It's a disease called numerosis, I'm told. By a strange coincidence it seems that BMWs proliferate most in the Midlands, none of them very new. Perhaps word's got around that the place is full of people who think they are reliable cars...

When it comes to brushes with the law I suppose I've had my quota of minor motoring misdemeanours – doing 50 in a 40mph zone, driving in a bus lane for 20 yards and other earth-shattering offences. But I can't cap the experience of a friend of mine. He's a solicitor and, coming out of a police club do after an evening with the lads in blue, he drove out of the carpark straight into the back of a panda car! (In the true spirit of British Justice he received a 12-month suspension, readers will be pleased to learn.)

RODIN'S
CATTLE·GRID

SWEAR
BOX

SELECT
LOW
GEAR

Larry

Stratford and Shakespeare

I first visited Stratford on a bike ride when I was 13 and I've now lived here for nearly ten years. Of course, the first thing you think of about the town is Shakespeare and this makes it a fairly active place both for the theatre and for visitors to the Bard's birthplace.

You can always tell which play is running at the Memorial Theatre by watching the pub types in the audience going across to the Dirty Duck (Black Swan) opposite afterwards. If they're strolling casually it's probably Macbeth *but if they're legging it you can bet it's* Hamlet. *It's more to do with the length of the play than the effect it has on those watching - if it's* Antony and Cleopatra *the pub's probably been shut for half an hour!*

Not being a great intellectual, a lot of Shakespeare goes over my head, but I enjoy the plays even if I understand only a part of them and anyway the accompanying orchestra always makes it worth a visit. And we've got some great actors. A lot live locally but some come only in the season. You can bump into Kenneth Branagh in Marks & Spencer's or some female lead going over her lines in the public gardens, while others try out fencing positions and shout 'Out, damn spot' to the ducks on the Avon. There's never a dull moment.

JUST *Larry*

I suppose this is really a sort of 'best of the rest' section. It's not that the cartoons are leftovers or anything, but just that they didn't really seem to fit neatly into any of the other categories.

It also gives me a chance to ramble on a bit about what I've been up to recently. In particular the small clay sculptures I've exhibited at the Chris Beetles Gallery and elsewhere.

They're actually 3D cartoons on art themes – usually poking fun at famous paintings like in the *Larry on Art* books. I haven't done the sunflowers yet but Van Gogh is a favourite subject. I've done the postman Rollin (plus attacking dog), Dr Gachet (with a gin and tonic), the church at Anvers (as a cheese dish) and more are planned. I've probably done about 30 different models so far. Whistler's mother with a bottle of Guinness seems popular, as is 'Pretty Little Rottweilers' (a spoof on Ford Madox Brown's 'Pretty Little Baa-lambs'), but to date my biggest success has been

my version of David's 'Death of Marat' – lying in his bath of blood with a rubber duck and model boat! I started off using self-hardening clay – red or white – but then I found I got a better result using ordinary modelling clay and getting a potter friend to fire it for me, painting on a coloured glaze. I don't draw them up beforehand, just whack the clay about on the table until it looks right. It has the advantage over paper that you can

move it about trying to get an arm
or a hand right – something that
would take several sheets of paper
if I tried to sketch it. Also, I always
draw very swiftly and rarely take
more than a few minutes over a
cartoon – someone once said (me,
I think) that I spend more time
on the signature than the drawing,
but of course it's years of experience... (yawn!). With clay, though,
I can spend a whole day or more on
a sculpture without killing the
thing off. If cartooning is 90 per
cent sitting and thinking and 10 per
cent drawing, then it's completely
t'other way about for clay
modelling.

They're mostly one-offs at the
moment. I've done plates and
things in the past – even bathroom
tiles based on my 'Man in Bath' jokes
– but they've always been transfer-
printed, and I've never been very
happy with the results. So who
knows, maybe this is
where I'm heading
next – serious
sculpture? Or
perhaps I
should move
into garden
gnomes…

THE END

" It says here it's by Rodin, better known as Larry "